尾田栄一郎

Here's volume 10. It's been two years since I started this series. Two years...two years... Back then Sazae-san, who's 24, was only 24... Oh, now that I think about it, I'm now the same age as Sazae-san. But it seems like I used to be the same age as Katsuo-kun. Who will it be next? Norisuke-kun? Taiko-san? Tara-san? It makes me laugh to say "Tara-san." Or "Ikura-san." What am I going on about? Anyway, I'm the same as ever—not working, just drawing manga.

-Eiichiro Oda, 1999

Editor's note: The aforementioned names belong to ageless characters from the beloved cartoon series, *Sazae-san*.

iichiro Oda began his manga career at the age of 17, when his one-shot cowboy manga **Wanted!** won second place in the coveted Tezuka manga awards. Oda went on to work as an assistant to some of the biggest manga artists in the industry, including Nobuhiro Watsuki, before winning the Hop Step Award for new artists. His pirate adventure **One Piece**, which debuted in **Weekly Shonen Jump** in 1997, quickly became one of the most popular manga in Japan.

ONE PIECE VOL. 10
EAST BLUE PART 10

SHONEN JUMP Manga Edition

This volume contains material that was originally
published in English in **SHONEN JUMP** #36–38.

STORY AND ART BY EIICHIRO ODA

English Adaptation/Lance Caselman
Translation/Naoko Amemiya
Touch-up Art & Lettering/Mark McMurray
Additional Touch-up/Josh Simpson
Design/Sean Lee
Editor/Yuki Takagaki

Printed in Italy

Published by VIZ Media, LLC
P.O. Box 77010
San Francisco, CA 94107

25
First printing, April 2006
Twenty-fifth printing, July 2024

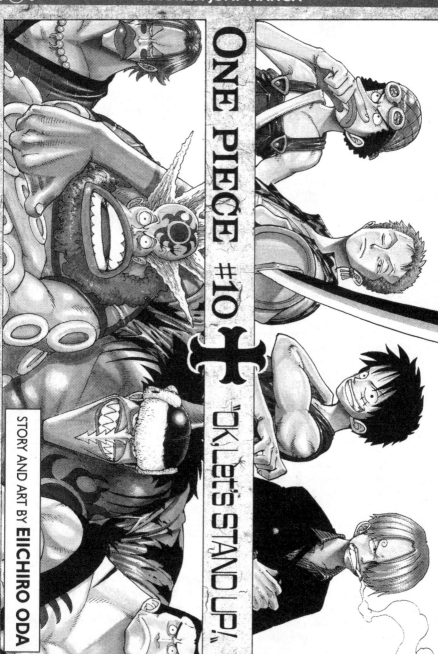

ONE PIECE #10

"OK, Let's STAND UP!"

STORY AND ART BY EIICHIRO ODA

Genzo

Nojiko

"Red-Haired" Shanks

THE STORY OF ONE PIECE
Volume 10

Monkey D. Luffy started out as just a kid with a dream — and that dream was to become the greatest pirate in history! Stirred by the tales of pirate "Red-Haired" Shanks, Luffy vowed to become a pirate himself. That was before the enchanted Devil Fruit gave Luffy the power to stretch like rubber, at the cost of being unable to swim — a serious handicap for an aspiring sea dog. Undeterred, Luffy set out to sea and recruited some crewmates: lying sharpshooter Usopp, master swordsman Zolo, and treasure-hunting thief Nami.

Luffy and his shipmates have finally defeated Don Krieg and his pirates and added the high-kicking cook Sanji to their crew. At last it seems they can finally set sail for the Grand Line—until they discover that their navigator, Nami, has deserted! Zolo and Usopp sail after her and come upon an island under the tyrannical rule of the fiendish Fish-Man Pirates and their leader, Captain "Saw-Tooth" Arlong. Worse still, Nami is in cahoots with them.

Luffy and the others reach the island, but despite what they hear about Nami they refuse to believe it. They come to understand Nami's hatred of pirates when they learn from her foster sister, Nojiko, that their adoptive mother, Belle-Mère, was killed by Arlong. They discover, too, that Nami has been hoarding her loot to buy Coco Village back from Arlong. Nami, who has been fighting a solitary battle for so long, finally asks Luffy for help.

Kuroobi

Sanji
The kind-hearted cook (and ladies' man) whose dream is to find the legendary sea, the "All Blue."

Hatchan (Hachi)

Nami
A thief who specializes in robbing pirates. Nami hates pirates, but Luffy convinced her to join his crew as navigator.

Monkey D. Luffy
Boundlessly optimistic and able to stretch like rubber, he is determined to become the King of the Pirates.

Roronoa Zolo
A former bounty hunter and master of the "three-sword" fighting style. He plans to become the world's greatest swordsman!

Usopp
A village boy with a talent for telling tall tales. His father, Yasopp, is a member of Shanks's crew.

Arlong

Choo

Vol. 10
OK, Let's STAND UP!

CONTENTS

EIICHIRO ODA

ONE PIECE

1 STAND BY

2 STAND BY

3 STAND THE PAIN

5 STAND BY

4 STAND BY

EPISODE 82 "OK, Let's STAND UP!"

YOU'D BETTER STOP...

SWUP

FIRST YOU GOTTA TELL US YOUR STORY.

HEH HEH HEH. STOP RIGHT THERE.

WHERE DO YOU THINK YOU'RE GOING?

AYE...

SHFF

SHFF SHFF

KR

OUTTA MY WAY.

!!?

WHAT BUSINESS DO YOU HAVE WITH ME, PIRATE?

SHFF SHFF SHFF

KERPLONES

HEY !!

!

YOU MUST BE CRAZY!!!

SH OOM!!!

HUMAN SCUM!

GRAAAH!!!

BAM BAM BAM BAM BAM

!!?

STAY OUT OF THIS, YOU CRAP-FISH!!!

YEAH, BUT I DON'T LOSE!!

YOU ALWAYS HAVE TO DIVE RIGHT IN, DON'T YOU?

I'M NOT WORRIED ABOUT THAT, DUMMY!!

TMP TMP

......!!

HOW GENEROUS OF YOU, USOPP...

I-IT'S OKAY WITH ME IF YOU DON'T SHARE, LUFFY.

JUST SAVE A LITTLE FOR THE REST OF US.

OKAY.

PIRATES, EH? SO THAT'S THE CONNECTION.

LONG NOSE IS ALIVE!!

I THOUGHT NAMI KILLED HIM!!

THAT'S THE GUY THAT TRICKED ME!!

RORONOA ZOLO!!

HE TOOK ME FOR A RIDE... I MEAN, I TOOK HIM FOR A RIDE!!

WHAT'S THIS!?

YOU SEE HIM SEND THAT MONSTER ARLONG FLYING!?

HE CAN'T BE A NORMAL HUMAN!!

YACK YACK

HEY!! JUST WHO ARE THOSE GUYS!?

IF YOU INSIST ON BUTTING INTO THIS FIGHT, YOU'LL HAVE TO GO THROUGH US!!

YOU'LL ONLY BE GETTING IN OUR COMRADES' WAY HERE.

YOU CAN'T DEFEAT THE FISH-MEN YOUR-SELVES.

THAT'S A GOOD ENOUGH REASON FOR US TO RISK OUR LIVES.

DO-OM!!

THEY MADE SISTER NAMI CRY.

DOOM!!

YOU HAVE NO REASON TO FIGHT!

WHY ARE YOU DOING THIS?

14

HA HA HA HA!! YOU'RE JUST FOUR PEOPLE FROM AN INFERIOR SPECIES.

WHAT CAN YOU DO!!?

YOU MEAN TO TELL ME...

...YOU CAME HERE FOR NAMI?

NO!!!

WHAT?

ARISE, GIANT WARRIOR !!!

TOOT-TOOT-TOOOT-TOOT-TOOOT!

DO YOU BONEHEADS THINK...

...YOU CAN PUSH LORD ARLONG AROUND? I'LL TURN YOU INTO CHUM!!!

OOOOO

ARLONG PARK

THE ONE THAT DECIMATED GOSA!!

THE MONSTER FROM THE GRAND LINE!!

AGH! WHAT IS IT!!?

AAAAH!

SPLOOSH

COME ON OUT, MOMOO !!!

PLUP···!!

MOO...

!

IT'S THE FEROCIOUS SEA COW, MOMOO!!!

HUH?

THE MONSTER!!! IT'S HERE!!

AAAAA

OH, IT'S JUST HIM.

SO HE WORKS FOR THESE GUYS.

WHERE ARE YOU GOING!!?

WAIT, MOMOO!!

MOO-HOO!!!

SWOOO.....SH

MOO...

WHAT DO YOU THINK YOU'RE DOING?

MOMOO?

I CAME HERE TO CLOBBER...

I DIDN'T COME HERE TO WASTE TIME ON SMALL FRY!!

... YOU!!!!

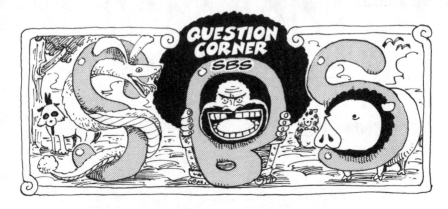

Q: This is Timmy Ueda of the SBS Takeover Gang!
I'm going to begin the SBS Question Corner before you do,
Oda Sensei!!
SBS will now begin!!

A: Agh! Oh no, you did it!
Darn you, Timmy.
Now I can't do it! Well, I guess it's already begun.

Q: Hello, Oda Sensei. On page 92 of volume 8, in panel
6, it says "Find Panda Man," but I can't find him.
Where is he?

A: Oh, that. I got a lot of postcards
about that. Some people found
him and some didn't. First of all,
I didn't even expect people to
notice those tiny words.
Nevertheless, I'll give the answer.
Inside the lower circle, it does
indeed say, "Find Panda Man!!!" And
Panda Man can be seen in the
circle at the upper right.

THANKS FOR THE BOAT. CAN WE KEEP IT?

KREEK...!!

SEE YOU AROUND.

WE'LL SINK !!

WE'LL SINK !!

(THE SCENE IN QUESTION)

Find Panda Man!!!

← Close-up, lower left

Close-up, upper right →

← He's making a peace sign.

Chapter 83:
LUFFY IN BLACK

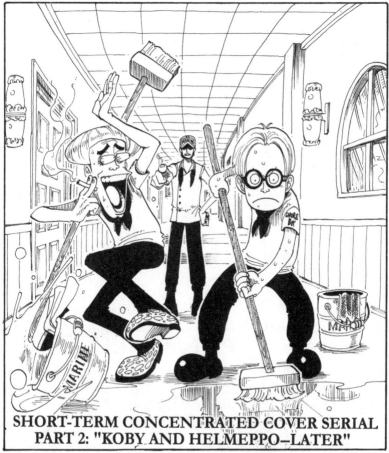

**SHORT-TERM CONCENTRATED COVER SERIAL
PART 2: "KOBY AND HELMEPPO–LATER"**

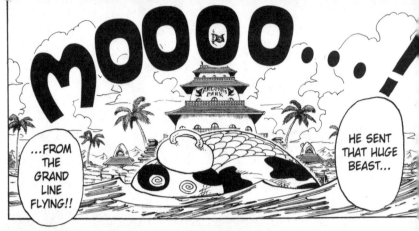

MOOOO...!

...FROM THE GRAND LINE FLYING!!

HE SENT THAT HUGE BEAST...

DO——OM!!

...INCREDIBLE POWER!

WHAT...

WOoOOOOO...

UN-BELIEVABLE !!

OOOOOO...

LET'S SEE WHAT THESE GUYS CAN DO.

VEEN

klik klikklik...

A HUMAN WHO'S A MATCH FOR THE FISH-MEN.

DA-DOOM!!

WE SHOULD'VE CRUSHED THESE HUMANS AS SOON AS THEY SHOWED UP!

I'VE ENTERED THE FRAY ON BEHALF OF THAT FOOL OF A CAPTAIN.

WHAT HAVE I DONE?

HOORAY, SANJI!

KA-BOOS

KLAK.

KLAK KLAK..

... HE'S NOT SO BAD!!

BUT HEY, COMPARED TO A BUNCH OF WOMAN-HATING CRAP-PIRATES ...

HE'S INCRED-IBLE!!

KLUNK!!

YOU SAID IT...

STILL ?

MY FEET STILL WON'T COME OUT!

HUH ?

...BUT THAT WAS A RATHER GALLANT ACT FOR A PIRATE.

YOU'RE PRETTY STRONG, FOR A HUMAN...

WAAAAH!!!

WHOOM

I'LL SMASH YOU!!!

C'MON, LUFFY! TRY POINTING YOUR TOES!!

TMP TMP TMP TMP TMP

!?

HEY, OCTOPUS.

THEY'RE BUSY RIGHT NOW.

KREK

KREK...!!

I ALMOST FORGOT ABOUT YOU!!

GRRR!!

RORONOA ZOLO!!

WHY DON'T YOU SMASH ME?

YOU MUST REALLY WANT ME TO HURT YOU!!

AAAAAAAH!!!

WAAAAAAH!!!

SHOOM!!

BROTHER USOPP!!

...!!

JUDGING FROM THE WEAPONS YOU'RE HOLDING...

AND THAT MEANS THAT EVERY ONE OF YOU HAS TO...

...I'D SAY THIS IS A REBELLION.

YOU'RE FROM COCO VILLAGE, AREN'T YOU?

SMEK. ♡

HEY, DIDN'T YOU GUYS COME HERE TO CHALLENGE US?

YOU'RE STILL HERE?

HE'S ONE OF THE PIRATES TOO?

ISN'T HE THE GUY THAT SAVED GENZO AT THE VILLAGE?

AAAAAH!!!!

WHOOSH!!...

OKAY, NOW YOU'RE REALLY A GONER!!!

...FIGHTING THE FISH-MEN!? A GUY LIKE THAT...

ONE MOMENT HE'S BRAVE, THE NEXT HE RUNS AWAY SCREAMING...

NO, HE'S JUST AN ODD ONE.

TMP TMP TMP TMP TMP

IS THERE SOMETHING WRONG WITH THAT YOUNG MAN!?

WOO OOO...

WAP!!

DO YOU FOOLS ACTUALLY THINK YOU CAN BEAT US?

...SOME-THING YOU WANT TO SAY?

IS THERE...

NOW LET GO OF MY HAND !!

DARN RIGHT WE DO !!

YEAH, WE ACTUALLY DO.

KRAK KRAK

KRAK

!?

WHAM!!

NO...NO THANKS!!

YOU BITER!!!

WHA...

FOOL...

BAM!

OW!!!

HE'S FINISH- ED.

....!!

SPLASH

HA HA HA HA HA!!

!!!

WAAH!!!?

HOLD ON!!

WAP!!

I'M COMING, LUFFY!!

WHY, YOU!!!

LUFFY!!

EXCELLENT PLAN.

FINISH THESE CUSTOMERS OFF, THEN DRAG HIM OUT?

THERE'S ONLY ONE WAY TO RESCUE LUFFY!!

JUMPING INTO THE OCEAN IS JUST WHAT THEY WANT US TO DO!!!

HA HA HA HA HA!!

TIME TO PLAY, EH?

YEAH!!!

LET'S DO IT!!!

KLANK!!

WOOOOOO

AAAAAH!!

GLUB GLUB

THIS IS BAD. I HAVE NO STRENGTH...

Q: When Arlong and the other Fish-Men have children, do they lay eggs like fish do?

A: (Buzz) The Fish-Men are actually mammals, so they have kids the same way humans do. Of course, that's the job of the Fish-Women.

Q: I, like, totally wanna know the heights of the crew. That Nami is, like, soooo cute!

A: The main five, eh? All right. Um, first of all, Gaimon's height is... Just kidding. Okay, I'll start with the shortest. Nami's 5' 6 ½", Luffy is 5' 8," Usopp is 5' 8 ½", Sanji is a little under 5' 10," and Zolo is 5' 10." So basically, they're all like about the same height.

Q: Of the Fish-Men, Hatchan is the cutest and funniest. So what I wonder is, how come his full name is Hatchan and his nickname is Hachi? (In Japanese, "-chan" is usually part of a nickname.)

A: You know how Chinese people sometimes have Chan as a last name? It's kind of the same thing.

Q: What is that thing wrapped around the waists of Usopp and most of the pirates that appear in *One Piece*? A towel? Or are they trying to copy Zolo's haramaki?

A: ◀ You mean this? Yeah, they're all wearing it, huh. But there's no deep significance to it. It's just a sash. It seems that pirates liked to wear them. But they used to stick pistols and knives in them, so they aren't just for show.

Chapter 84:
ZOMBIE

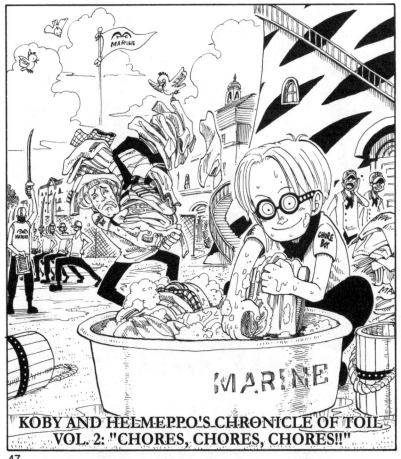

KOBY AND HELMEPPO'S CHRONICLE OF TOIL
VOL. 2: "CHORES, CHORES, CHORES!!"

SH WU

!!!!?

SWOOSH

EEK!!! MY HAIR!!!

HMPH.

UM... THANKS?

...YOU'RE ABSOLUTELY RIGHT!!! HEY, IT'S ONLY HAIR! IT'LL GROW BACK!!

GR

IF YOU THINK I'LL LET YOU GET AWAY WITH THAT...

HUMAN SCUM!!!

52

GLUB

THE PAIN!! MY LUNGS ARE BURSTING!!

...!!

GLUB

TUM ...P!!

SEE, RORONOA ZOLO!? I'M MORE THAN A MATCH FOR ANY SWORDSMAN.

NOW DO YOU GET IT!?

RUM

WWWMBB

FWASH!!

WHOOM!

YEAH, YOU TALK A LOT!!!

SWORD CATCH!!!

HACHI'S TRIPLE ...

GRRRR
RRR...

TUK...
TUK...
TUK...

FOO
!

MII

I HEARD YOU USE A THREE-SWORD STYLE.

STOP STALLING!!!

WHAT THE HECK!? GET DOWN HERE!!!

...

DA—DOOM

SO WHY ONLY ONE SWORD!?

SHUT UP!! I'M NOT EVEN TRYING!!!

YOU'RE LOSING PLENTY AGAINST JUST ONE SWORD, FISH!!

GLUB

GLUB

... A HUMAN SWORDS-MAN CAN NEVER BEAT ME !!!

THERE'S A REASON WHY...

WE'VE GOT TO DO SOME-THING TO SAVE HIM!!

BUT AT THIS RATE, BROTHER LUFFY'S DOOMED!!

BUT IF WE DIVE INTO THE OCEAN NOW, THEY'LL JUST DRAG US TO THE BOTTOM!!

DARN!! THAT SLIPPERY OCTOPUS CLOWN IS WASTING OUR PRECIOUS TIME!!

MR. GENZO...

I'LL GO HELP THAT YOUNG RUBBER BOY.

YOU THINK YOU CAN ACCOMPLISH ANYTHING IN THE OCEAN, INJURED LIKE YOU ARE!?

BUT...

KL-IK

KL-IK...

THROB

THROB

OUCH !!!

WAIT FOR US!!

TUP!

ZING!!

AND ME !!

COUNT ME IN!

ME TOO, MR. GENZO.

I'LL GO, TOO !!

BUT, MR. GENZO!

I'LL GO ALONE!!

...AND THE RUBBER BOY AND HIS FRIENDS WILL HAVE FOUGHT FOR NOTHING.

THAT'S AN ORDER.

IF THE FISH-MEN SPOT A CROWD OF US IN THE WATER, THEY'LL ATTACK...

NO!!

IT'S MY LITTLE SISTER THOSE GUYS ARE FIGHTING FOR!

NOJIKO!! BUT YOUR STOMACH...

MR. GENZO, I'M GOING TOO!!

WE'LL LEAVE YOU TO IT! BUT HURRY!

GOOD LUCK !!

HUH !?

AH HA HA HA!

HUFF...

HUFF...

AAAAAGH!!!

I'LL CRUSH YOU.

I THOUGHT IT WAS STRANGE THAT HE COULD GET CUT UP LIKE THAT AND RECOVER SO FAST!!

THAT STUPID IDIOT.

OF COURSE! THEY WOULD'VE KILLED ANY NORMAL MAN-- OR AT LEAST CRIPPLED HIM FOR HALF A YEAR!!

SO THOSE WOUNDS WERE TOO DEEP, AFTER ALL...

OUR BROTHER'S BEEN SUFFERING IN SILENCE ALL THIS TIME!!

FWUMP!!

twitch

CRAP...

WHY NOW OF ALL TIMES!?

... FIGHTING MAD NOW! LET ME AT 'IM !!!

KRASH!!

GRRAAAR!!! THIS OCTOPUS-MAN IS...

HOW LONG ARE YOU GONNA SLEEP!?

HACHI!! WAKE UP!!

NO MERE HUMAN COULD EVER BEAT ME, EVEN IF HEAVEN AND EARTH TURNED UPSIDE DOWN !!!

I'M THE SECOND BEST SWORDS-MAN ON FISH-MAN ISLAND!! THEY CALL ME HACHI OF THE SIX-SWORD STYLE!!! DID YOU KNOW THAT!!?

SIX-SWORD STYLE? SOUNDS SILLY.

IS THAT FOR CHOPPING VEGETABLES!?

WHO ARE YOU GOING TO FIGHT, HACHI?

HUH?

HUH!!?

LISTEN UP, OCTOPUS!!

...NO ONE CAN TAKE MY LIFE!!!

THERE'S A MAN I HAVE TO MEET, AND UNTIL I SEE HIM AGAIN...

I'LL KILL YOU, RORONOA ZOLO!!!

HE'S ALIVE, EH?

YEAH, ZOLO!!!

NOW I'LL SHOW YOU THE THREE-SWORD STYLE.

YOSAKU, JOHNNY...YOUR SWORDS!

HMPH. THAT'S IT?

WHP WHP

TUMP!!

GULP...!!

...!!

EWIK

...THEN THOSE KICKS THE CRAP-GEEZER USED TO LAY ON ME MUST'VE BEEN 400TH DEGREE.

DO

OMM!!

PLIP...

IF THAT WAS A 40TH-DEGREE PUNCH...

TMP TMP

AAAAAAAAAAH!!!

GLUB

!

GLUB

Q: Here goes! Oooone! Twoooo!! Threeeee!!!

A: Thump!!!!

Q: One more time! ♡ Oooone. ♡ Twoooo. ♡ Threeeee. ♡

A: Thump!!! Oh...I'm being played.

Q: Yo! Wassup? ONE PIECE is A-OK! It's always lots of fun and a regular storm of emotions. This is my first time writing to a manga artist. ♡ Oda Sensei, you're a character I like.

A: I'm not a character.

Q: The other day a friend asked me to draw Shanks, so I did. Then suddenly my friend hit me on the head and said, "How come you drew Django!?" Am I sick?

A: Yes. It's an illness. It's "Django Drawer's Disease." You just keep drawing Django. Late-stage symptoms include drawing Django even when you're signing for deliveries, so please be careful.

Q: That thing that's perched on Zeff's head on page 121 of volume 8 is a hat, right? My mom won't believe me. She says, "It's too tall to be a hat. There must be a pole behind him." Sensei, please tell her yourself so the blockhead (age 44) will believe it.

A: Er, Mom, please listen carefully. In this world, there are facts that cannot be bent and realities from which we cannot avert our eyes. The thing that looms above Zeff's head is a "Tower of Faith" that rises up because of his spirit. It is called the "Blue Heavens-Dividing Chef's Hat!" It's true!!!!

Chapter 85:
THREE SWORDS VS. SIX

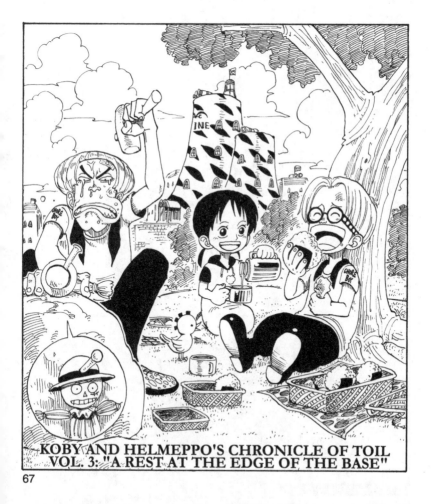

KOBY AND HELMEPPO'S CHRONICLE OF TOIL
VOL. 3: "A REST AT THE EDGE OF THE BASE"

ONLY BROTHER ZOLO CAN CLEAN UP THIS ISLAND!!

BUT THERE'S NO TIME TO WORRY ABOUT THAT.

WHUP!!

IF THOSE WOUNDS OPEN NOW...

...HE'LL DIE FOR SURE...

BROTHER ZOLO'S IN BAD SHAPE!!

HIS WOUNDS HAVE MADE HIM FEVERISH!

DO

On.

RORONOA ZOLO, YOU LOOK LIKE A WALKING CORPSE, AND I HAVEN'T EVEN STARTED ON YOU YET.

SWFF

TVN

K...!!

KEEP YOUR COMMENTS TO YOUR-SELF.

FWIP

FWIP

FWIP FWIP

WHOOSH!!

CATCH, BROTHER !!!

WE THREW THEM TO YOU!! CATCH THEM!!!

FWIP FWIP FWIP FWIP

BROTHER!! OUR SWORDS!!

THIS IS BAD... I'M ABOUT TO PASS OUT. AND MY FEVER, INSTEAD OF GOING DOWN, IS RISING!!

HUFF... HUFF...

BROTHER ZOLO, LOOK OUT!!!

FWIP FWIP

FWIP FWIP

Wobble   Wobble

THIS IS THE **SIX-SWORD** STYLE, WHICH CAN ONLY BE PERFORMED BY SOMEONE WITH SIX ARMS AND A CHARMINGLY FLEXIBLE BODY.

I'LL SHOW YOU A WORLD THAT NO TWO-ARMED HUMAN CAN ENTER !!!

JUST THINK ABOUT IT MATHE-MATICALLY. THREE BLADES...

...IS THE MAXIMUM YOU CAN HOLD. YOU HAVE NO CHANCE AGAINST MY SIX BLADES.

I'M GOING TO CHOP YOU UP !!!

WHY DO YOU FIGHT SO HARD WHEN YOU CANNOT WIN?

WHAT DRIVES YOU?

THAT WOULD BE A GRAVE MISCALCU-LATION.

MATHEMA-TICALLY !?

THEY'RE MUCH WEIGHTIER THAN YOURS ARE!!!

I MAY ONLY HAVE THREE BLADES, BUT LOOK AT THEM!

WO oo o OoOC

DARN IT! I DON'T KNOW IF THIS WILL WORK ON THE OCEAN FLOOR!!!

THE WATER'S BUOYANCY IS TOO STRONG!!

KLANG

GLUG

GLUG

KLANG !!

HE'S SWALLOWED AN AWFUL LOT OF WATER!! IF WE CAN'T FREE HIM SOON, IT'LL BE TOO LATE!!

GLUG

KLANG

GLUG

I NEED AN OXYGEN TANK, BUT THERE'S NO TIME TO GET ONE!!

AND I CAN'T CARRY HIM TO THE SURFACE WITH THE THING ATTACHED!!

THAT'S IT!!

GLUG

IT'S NO USE! I CAN'T BREAK THE ROCK!!!

HURRY!

MR. GENZO...

WHAT
!!?

!!

EEEYOUCH
!!!

KLANG KLANG

KLANG...

FWOOSH!!!

THIS TECHNIQUE IS 100% UNSTOPPABLE!!!

IT ALREADY WORKED ON YOU ONCE!!!

EVEN IF THESE WOUNDS WOULD KILL MOST PEOPLE...

...I CANNOT DIE.

WHEEZE

KLA-KL

NEW YEAR'S...

ANG!!!

--GIRI!!!

I HAVE TO LIVE TO DEFEAT "HAWK-EYE" MIHAWK.

I CANNOT FALL.

SW

UP...

ONI--

SRIK

SRIK...

HUH...?

EH, OCTOPUS BOY!? ARE YOU SATISFIED!?

NOW DO YOU SEE WHOSE SWORDS ARE WEIGHTIER?

DRAGON...

HE COULDN'T HAVE...

HACHI...

HOW... COULD I LOSE TO ONLY THREE SWORDS?

WHA-KRASH!!!

THE REST OF YOU ARE BENEATH MY NOTICE.

I HAVE TO SAVE LUFFY!!

KLAK

RORONOA ZOLO!! HOW DARE YOU DO THAT TO HACHI!!?

RRM MM BBB

HMPH... I NEVER THOUGHT THERE WAS A HUMAN IN THE EAST BLUE WHO COULD TAKE THE FULL FORCE OF MY PUNCH AND LIVE.

BROTHER COOK...

YOU SENT ME FLYING QUITE A WAYS BEFORE...

ESPECIALLY AT A CERTAIN RESTAURANT I KNOW.

YOU UNDER-ESTIMATE ME.

AW, I'LL WAGER THERE ARE LOTS WHO COULD DO IT.

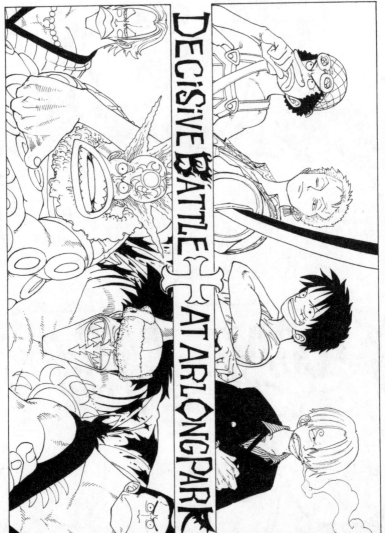

Chapter 86:
HEROISM VS.
FISH-MAN CRUELTY

STOP, ZOLO!!

IF YOU GO INTO THE OCEAN LIKE THAT YOU'LL DIE!!

!

WHUP···!!!

WHEEZE

HAVE TO HURRY... LUFFY...

I CAN'T WAIT AROUND FOR YOU TO FIGHT!!

I KNOW!!

WHEEZE

WHEEZE

SHUT UP!! LUFFY'S GOT TO BE AT HIS LIMIT BY NOW!!

!?

I'M STOPPING YOU BECAUSE I KNOW THAT ALL TOO WELL, CRAP-SWORDSMAN!!

I KNOW THERE'S NO TIME.

YOU IDIOT!

SO YOU CAN'T BLAME ME FOR DOING THIS, RIGHT!!?

THAT'S EXACTLY WHAT THESE GUYS WANT!!!

THAT RECKLESS IDIOT!!

INTERESTING!! HE WANTS TO FIGHT ME, A FISH-MAN, UNDERWATER!!?

AH HA HA HA HA HA!

WHAT AN INCREDIBLE FOOL!!

BWAH HA HA HA HA!!! LEARN THIS LESSON WELL!! YOU HUMANS ARE NO MATCH FOR US!!!

WHAT!? ISN'T THAT...

...THE VILLAGE HEADMAN!!?

!?

DO

Om!!

GLUB

GLUB

IS THAT LUFFY'S STRETCHED NECK!?

HURRY, BEFORE MY BREATH RUNS OUT...

WUMP

WUMP

PLEASE LET US BE IN TIME!!!

C'MON, BREATHE!!

WHUMP

WHUMP

...WITH THIS STRETCHY NECK OF YOURS, YOU COULD AT LEAST COUGH UP WATER AND BREATHE!!

I'M SORRY!! I DON'T HAVE THE STRENGTH TO BRING UP YOUR WHOLE BODY, BUT...

THAT'S IT, MR. GENZO!!

YES!!

PLOOSH

WHUMP

WHUMP

...AND LEAVE THE REST TO THE OLD MAN!!

GLUB GLUB

THEN I JUST HAVE TO SHATTER THE ROCK WITH A KICK...

GLUB

GOOD. NOW EVEN WITH HIS FEET IN THE ROCK, HE CAN AT LEAST BREATHE!!

GLUB

FISH-
MAN
KARATE
...

FOREARM
SLEDGE
!!!

!!!?

HMPH,
IT'S THOSE
WORMS
FROM COCO
VILLAGE!
BUT THEY'RE
WASTING
THEIR TIME
!!

BLOOP!!

...!!!

!?

I'LL
DROWN
YOU
RIGHT
NOW
!!!

GLUB
GLUB
GLUB

DO YOU
REALLY
THINK YOUR
EFFORTS...

...WILL
BUY YOU
ANY MORE
TIME IN
THIS
WORLD
!?

I'VE
BEEN
SPOTTED
BY A
FISH-
MAN!!

GLUB

OH
NO
!!

GLUB

THWAP!!

NOT IF I CAN HELP IT!!

IT'LL BE ALL YOU CAN DO JUST TO HOLD YOUR BREATH, HUMAN!!

YOU WANT TO FIGHT *ME* UNDERWATER!?

...!!

WHAP!!

!?

THE DUELLING HAIR TETHER!!!

ALL RIGHT, THEN. I'LL TAKE YOU ON!!

HMPH. THAT WAS WEAK. DOWN HERE YOUR KICKS HAVE HALF THE FORCE THEY'D HAVE ON LAND.

BUT WITH FISH-MAN KARATE, THERE'S NO LOSS OF POWER IN THE WATER.

SWUP...

BLOOSHH!!!

WAAK!!!!

BOWEL-BUSTER!!!

INSTANT UNDER-SEA...

IN FACT, THE POWER OF SOME MOVES IS EVEN MULTIPLIED!!

GLUB GLUB GLUB

!

FWRR R RRR

GLUB

FLAMING AXE KICK !!!

GLUB ...!!

KRAK!!

BACK FOOT JAW-BREAKER !!!

....!!

UNGH!! I LET OUT TOO MUCH AIR!! I NEED AIR! AIR!!

BOOM!

SW OO H!!

WHERE ARE *YOU* GOING?

PLOOF !!!

YOUR ABILITY TO TAKE PUNISHMENT IS ANNOYING. IT'S NOT NORMAL FOR A HUMAN.

CRAP!!! LET ME PASS!!! AIR!!! I GOTTA BREATHE !!!

YOU WANT TO ESCAPE FROM ME, BUT YOU CAN'T.

GLUB

THIS GAME ENDS IN ONLY ONE WAY... DEATH.

GLUB

BUT LET ME EXPLAIN TO YOU THE CONSEQUENCES OF YOUR FOOLHARDY HEROISM!!!

!!

THEN I'LL FINISH OFF THAT LONG-NOSED FOOL AND ZOLO, AND I'LL KILL ALL THE VILLAGERS FOR THEIR REBELLION!!

THE RUBBER MAN WILL DIE AT THE SAME TIME.

...!!

AND WHEN YOU'RE FINISHED, I'LL KILL THE VILLAGE HEADMAN.

IN THE END, YOUR HEROISM IS JUST SO MUCH HOT AIR.

TREMBLE...

IT CAN'T SAVE A SINGLE SOUL!!!

!!!!

AND AFTER ALL THIS, I CAN'T VERY WELL LET THAT TRAITOR NAMI GET AWAY, CAN I!!?

DO YOU UNDER-STAND?

...YOUR GUTS WOULD BE SQUEEZED OUT OF YOUR BODY!!!

IF YOU WERE TO DESCEND RAPIDLY TO THE BOTTOM OF THE OCEAN...

YOU CAN'T EVEN ENDURE EXTREME CHANGES IN WATER PRESSURE!!

SHWAP···!!

YOU HUMANS TRULY ARE POWERLESS CREATURES.

!

THE OLD MAN WILL HAVE TO TAKE CARE OF LUFFY FOR NOW.

GOTTA CHANGE THE PLAN!!

WOOS

PULVERIZING PRESSURE PLUNGE!!!

PLUNK

AH HA HA HA HA !!!

HE THINKS I CAN'T SAVE ANYONE!?

I WON'T LET HIM GET AWAY WITH THIS!!!

AND WHAT HAPPENED TO SISTER NAMI'S SISTER AND THAT MAN!?

BROTHER COOK'S NOT COMING UP!

THIS FOOL'S STILL NOT DEAD!?

...BREATHE WITH THEIR LUNGS ON LAND AND SWITCH TO GILLS IN THE WATER!! SO RIGHT NOW, HE'S JUST A TALKING FISH!!

FWAP

OM!!

ALL RIGHT THEN, WE'LL DO IT AGAIN !!!

THESE FISH-MEN...

FISH DIE WHEN AIR IS FORCED THROUGH THEIR GILLS!!

FWOOO!!

!?

WE'RE NEAR THE SURFACE NOW. THINK YOU CAN SURVIVE A SECOND PLUNGE?

FWOOOO

GWAAAGH !!!!

AND IT SHOULD BE THE SAME WITH HIM !!!

HALF !?

HALF OF HIM.

HE IS?

DON'T WORRY... HE'S ALL RIGHT.

I'LL EXPLAIN LATER !!!

HAAAAH!!! GASP!!! HAAGABAAAGAH !!!!

SANJI !!

HUH?

I'M GOING TO FINISH YOU !!!!

COME ON OUT HERE, YOU LOUSY FISH !!!

I'M MANY TIMES STRONGER THAN YOU ARE. IT DOESN'T MATTER IF WE'RE IN WATER OR OUT OF IT.

KOFF!! YOU STILL DON'T UNDERSTAND.

KOFF!!

AND NOW YOU'VE MADE ME MAD.

SPLASHHH......!!

BUT MY GREATEST MOVE IS THE THOUSAND-BRICK FIST. THE LIKELIHOOD OF YOUR SURVIVAL IS...ZERO!!!

I SENT YOU FLYING BEFORE WITH THE HUNDRED-BRICK FIST.

WO O O

I'LL DESTROY YOU WITH THE ULTIMATE MOVE OF FISH-MAN KARATE.

COLLIER* COUP !!!

WHA HA !!!

!!?

!

*COLLIER IS THE FRENCH TERM FOR "NECK MEAT."

ÉPAULE*
SPRAWL
!!!

ARGGH
!!!?

OOF
!!!

*EPAULE = SHOULDER. (NOTE: THE ASTERISKS ON THIS PAGE INDICATE FRENCH WORDS.)

THUD
!!!

BAM
!!!

CÔTELETTE*
KABOSH
!!!

WHAT DID
YOU SAY
YOU'D DO
TO ME!?

SELLE*
DE
OUCH
!!!

*SELLE = SADDLE (AS IN "SADDLE OF MUTTON")

*CÔTELETTE = BACK

*GIGOT = THIGH

*POITRINE = BREAST MEAT

GIGOT*
CHARLIE-
LE-HORSE
!!!

KA-

......!!!

POITRINE*
TREADER
!!!

AAAGH
!!

BASH
!!!

THOMP
!!!

THE ULTIMATE PUNCH, *THE THOUSAND-BRICK--*

...HUMAN!!

WOOSH!!

KRÉK KRÉK

WHY, YOU LITTLE...!!!

-BA-BA-BA-

MOUTON* MALLET!!!!

B

*MOUTON = LAMB

I GUESS YOU WON'T BE NEEDING DESSERT.

OO-OO-O OO...

Chapter 87:
IT'S ALL OVER!!

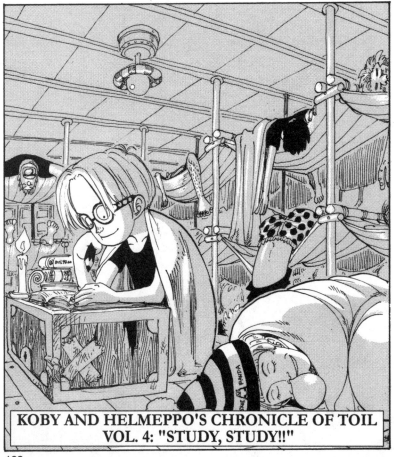

**KOBY AND HELMEPPO'S CHRONICLE OF TOIL
VOL. 4: "STUDY, STUDY!!"**

DOOM!!

HACHI
...

DO OM!!

KUROOBI
...

LOOKS LIKE WE'RE THE WINNERS OF THIS GAME.

DA-DOOM!!

LIKE I SAID, INSIGNIF-ICANT SMALL FRY.

KLAK

!!

HOW DARE YOU WIPE OUT MY MOST VALUABLE OFFICERS !?

WHO DO YOU THINK YOU ARE !!!?

IT MEANS HE'S NOT DEAD... YET.

I'LL HAVE TO GO BACK DOWN TO THE OCEAN FLOOR.

YOU SAID LUFFY'S HALF-OKAY.

WHAT'S THAT MEAN?

WHEEZE WHEEZE

KLAK

...THAT GUY ISN'T ABOUT TO LET ME.

BUT IT LOOKS LIKE...

THOSE GUYS ARE INCREDIBLE! THEY DEFEATED TWO OF ARLONG'S BEST MEN!!

......!!

HE'S COUGHING UP WATER. WE'RE SO CLOSE!

TAKE A BREAK, MR. GENZO!! I'LL GO DOWN NOW!!

HAAAH!! HAAAH!! THAT'S IT! I CAN'T HOLD MY BREATH ANY LONGER!!

GASP!

SPLASH!!

I STILL CAN HARDLY BELIEVE IT, BUT ...

I WAS AFRAID TO BELIEVE IT UNTIL NOW.

NOBODY'S BEEN KILLED, YET!! IN FACT...

HOW'S IT GOING OVER THERE!?

... ABOUT THIS BATTLE !!!

I FEEL A RISING SENSE OF HOPE ...

DOOM!!

DOOM!!

AND YOU WERE PRETTY FAST, FOR A HUMAN!!

BUT THEN YOU DIED FROM ONE SHOT OF MY LIP-O-BLASTER. HOW DISAPPOINTING.

SMEK! ♡ YOU GAVE ME A HARD CHASE.

MY COMRADES SHOULD BE FINISHED BY NOW TOO.

TMP
TMP

GUESS I'LL HEAD BACK...

THAT GUY THINKS HE HIT ME WITH HIS *LIP-O-BLISTER* THING!! HEE HEE...JUST KEEP WALKING, LIPS!!

plip...

SUCCESS!! I'M SAVED!! GOOD THING I MADE THOSE KETCHUP STARS FOR JUST THIS KIND OF SITUATION !!

TMP
TMP

BA-BUMP BLINK BA-BUMP BA-BUMP

I DO FEEL SORRY FOR NAMI...

...AND I WISH I COULD DO MORE TO HELP, BUT IF IT MEANS GETTING KILLED, I'LL PASS.

SHEESH, BUT WHAT A TERRIFYING SPECIES THEY ARE.

THEY CAN FLIP HOUSES UPSIDE DOWN! A WHOLE VILLAGE OF 'EM!!

tmp tmp

...THEN I MIGHT LOOK LIKE I FOUGHT A REAL BATTLE!

THAT'S IT! IF I SMEAR DIRT ALL OVER MYSELF...

...I WISH I HAD...A FEW MORE BATTLE SCARS!!

I'M COVERED WITH KETCHUP BLOOD, BUT...

RUB

RUB

WHAT SHOULD I SAY WHEN I GET BACK?

UMM, DON'T CRY, NAMI. IT WAS A HOPELESS BATTLE.

UMM, I ALMOST HAD HIM, BUT HE GOT AWAY.

WE'RE A TEAM, AREN'T WE?

UMM, SORRY. I LOST.

RUB

RUB

RUB

RUB

IT'S BUSINESS. I HAD NO CHOICE.

BUT HEY, COMPARED TO A BUNCH OF WOMAN-HATING CRAP PIRATES, HE'S NOT SO BAD!!

UMM, WELL, WE ALL PUT UP A GOOD FIGHT.

I PREFER DEATH TO DEFEAT.

UMM, WOW, THAT WAS ONE TOUGH FIGHT!

CAN YOU UNDERSTAND WHAT A PAINFUL CHOICE THAT WAS FOR HER?

WE'VE BEEN WAITING FOR YOU, BROTHERS!!!

UMM, MY WOUNDS AREN'T THAT BAD!!

......!!

RUB...

RUB....

......

RUB...

RUB...

RUB...!!

UMM, YOU SHOULDA SEEN ME FIGHT...

LET'S FIGHT!!!

THIS IS SHAMEFUL!!!!

SWIP

SHAKE

SHAKE
SHAKE

TOMP

LUFFY AND THOSE GUYS LIVE EVERY DAY LIKE THERE'S NO TOMORROW!!

YOU THINK I'D LET YOU HIT ME WITH YOUR WIMPY HALF-FISH SQUIRT GUN!!?

THE MOMENT I DECIDED TO LEAVE MY VILLAGE, I SAID GOODBYE TO PEACE AND SECURITY!!

SHAKE

SHAKE

SHAKE

!

BECAUSE I WANTED TO LAUGH WITH GUSTO, LIKE THEM !!!

ERK.... !

THAT'S THE REASON I SET OUT TO SEA IN THE FIRST PLACE!!

THAT'S WHY THEY CAN LAUGH SO HEARTILY!!

KREEEK!!

IF I DON'T FIGHT WITH EVERYTHING I'VE GOT...

HOW COULD I EVER LAUGH WITH THEM AGAIN !!?

...THEN I'M NOT WORTHY TO SAIL ON THE SAME SHIP WITH THOSE GUYS!!!

DEATH BLOW !!

FIRE STAR !!!

YOU THINK THAT'S GONNA STOP ME?

FW UMP...!!

YOUR BRAIN MUST BE AS WEAK AS YOUR BODY.

SMEK. ♥

YOU SHOULD'VE JUST PLAYED DEAD.

PLIP

PLIP.

THWAK THWAK

UNGH !!

AGH!

THWAK THWAK THWAK !!!

THAT'S RIGHT. IT'S ALL OVER FOR YOU !!!

IT'S ALL OVER.

twitch

twitch

... HAMMER !!!

USOPP'S ...

WHAK!!!

!!!

RUSTLE

IT'S ALL OVER.

SMEK?

KRAK...

OOF!!!

.....

.....!!

FLINCH!!

DOOM!!

SKREEK

USOPP'S RUBBER BAND OF DOOM !!!

THE LITTLE COWARD.

BA—DOOM!!!

GRAAAAAH!!

HE RAN AWAY!!

WHAT!!? THE FOOL TRICKED ME!!

WHAP...!!

BOOZE!?

FURRR R!!

!! SPURT

BL OOSH!!!

SHUNK!!

THE DEADLY LEAD STAR !!!

UGH !!!

SPURT

...I'LL BLAST YOU WITH THE WATER FROM THIS PADDY!!!

SMEK. ♡

SHLURRR

BUT NO MATTER WHERE YOU'RE HIDING...

GRR!! THIS PUNY HUMAN IS FULL OF INSOLENT TRICKS!!

WHUP...!!

PLIP...

SMEK. ♡

I'M A PIRATE NOW!!

IF I LOSE, I DIE!!

huff...

WHATEVER HAPPENS, I, USOPP, WILL NOT RUN FROM THIS FIGHT!!!

THAT FISH CAN SAY WHATEVER HE WANTS!

BOOM!!

LIP-O-CANNON!!!!

124

KA-BLOOSH!!!

KRAK KRAK

KREK KREK !!!

THWUMP!

WOW!!!

WHAT POWER!!!

DO—OM

SCARY

THERE HE IS.

WHY DO I HAVE TO FIGHT *THIS* FOOL?

Q: Sensei! I thought up a new technique for Luffy. He stretches his mouth and eats up his enemy and later flushes him down the toilet along with his *oop! What do you think? Good idea, huh?

A: It stinks-o.

Q: I've got a question for Oda Sensei. Whaddaya call Belle-Mère's hairdo?

A: It's called "women are brave." Go to the beauty parlor and shout it out.

Q: I'm glad that brother Sanji is a ladies' man and not a "gentlemen's man."

A: Indeed.

Q: When Sanji is thinking about a girl, his cigarette smoke forms the shape of a heart. How does he do that? I want to do that too!! Please (x100) teach me!

A: Hmm. First you have to be over 20 years old. Then light a cigarette and take a deep puff of smoke. Let the smoke soak up the feelings of love that you've prepared in your lungs and exhale it from your mouth. The smoke will surely come out in the shape of a heart.

Q: I can't quite decide whether Yosaku and Johnny are strong or not. I'm within a frog's hair of being able to tell. But really, between those two and Helmeppo, who will develop more?

A: I have high hopes that, one day, Kaya will become an excellent doctor.

Chapter 88:
DIE!!!

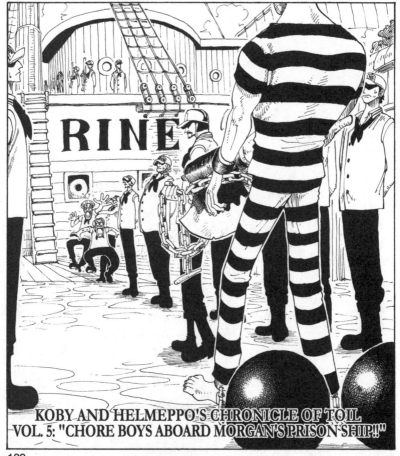

KOBY AND HELMEPPO'S CHRONICLE OF TOIL
VOL. 5: "CHORE BOYS ABOARD MORGAN'S PRISON SHIP!!"

SH

OOM!

HAMMER!!!!

.....

HUMF HUMF

SP LA — SH!!

SSSSS — SS!!

USOPP'S HAMMER!!

USOPP'S RUBBER BAND OF DOOM!!!

USOPP'S HAMMER!

USOPP'S HAMMER!

USOPP'S HAMMER!

WHAM! ... WHAK! BAM BAM!!

!!
.....

!!!!?

TWITCH!!

WHY... YOU...

I BEAT ...

haah haah haah
huff huff huff
haah huff ....!!

HUFF HUFF .....

SEE?

THWUMP...!!

HUFF

WHEEZE

klak klak shake HUFF ...A FISH-MAN!!

shake

I WON...

HUFF..

DON'T EVER UNDER-ESTIMATE ME!!!!

EVEN I CAN WIN IF I TRY!!! DID YOU SEE THAT, DARN IT!!?

SWIP...?

I'VE DONE MY CRYING!!

AND I'VE VOICED MY COMPLAINTS!!

KRK

UNH!!

MY MIND IS MADE UP!!

TMP TMP TMP TMP TMP

...AND JOIN THE FIGHT!!!

I HAVE TO GO...

...BUT THEN THEY COUGHED UP BLOOD AND COLLAPSED!!

I DON'T KNOW. IT LOOKED LIKE HE JUST SPLASHED THEM WITH WATER...

WHOA... WHAT DID THAT NASTY SHARK DO?

WAS IT ALL A DREAM!?

GLUB GLUB ...!!

WHUMP

WHUMP

BREATHE !!

PLEASE ...

SPLUP !!

WHAT'S HAPPENED TO BROTHER LUFFY!? HE COULDN'T HAVE DIED, COULD HE?

BROTHER COOK!! STAY DOWN!!

DID HE MOVE !?

JUST A LITTLE MORE !!!

TWITCH....

COME BACK TO LIFE!! PLEASE!!!

STAGGER ....

ACK !!

.....!!!

WHUMP !!!

WHUMP !!!

WHUMP

BUT HE'S LIKE A SHOTGUN BLAST!!! SO THIS IS THE POWER OF A SHARK...EVEN AMONG THE FISH-MEN, HE'S IN A CLASS BY HIMSELF!!

THIS GUY'S... NO JOKE!! HE MAKES IT LOOK EASY.

KOFF!

ACK !!!

YOUR LIVES ARE WORTH-LESS.

GO AHEAD AND DIE.

THIS IS LIKE NOTHING WE'VE FACED SO FAR!!

DO ZOMM!!

ARLONG !!!!

NAMI ...

SISTER NAMI !!

WHAT BRINGS YOU HERE?

I WAS JUST ABOUT TO BLAST THIS NO-ACCOUNT PIRATE TO BITS.

MISS NAMI... ♥

NAMI ...

...TO KILL YOU !!!

I'VE COME ...

ASSASSINS... POISON... AMBUSHES...

...HOW MANY TIMES DID YOU TRY TO KILL ME?

·······!!

!

BWAH HA HA HA HA HA !! BWAHHAHAHAHAHA

TO KILL ME !?

IN THE EIGHT YEARS YOU'VE BEEN WITH US...

YOU, OF ALL PEOPLE, SHOULD KNOW THAT NO MERE HUMAN CAN KILL ME!!!

AND THE RESULT!? I'M STILL HERE, AIN'T I!!?

!!!

SHIVER

YOU'RE GOING TO BE MY LITTLE CARTOGRAPHER FOREVER.

BUT I WON'T LET YOU GO !!!

NOW LISTEN. I'M NOT GOING TO KILL YOU...

I'D PREFER THAT YOU KEEP WORKING FOR ME OF YOUR OWN FREE WILL.

BUT I'M A REASONABLE FISH-MAN!

I DON'T WANT TO HOLD A YOUNG GIRL AGAINST HER WILL.

...IF YOU'RE WILLING TO REJOIN MY CREW...

...AND AGREE TO BE AN OFFICER AND DRAW OCEAN CHARTS...

...EXCEPT FOR YOU. HOWEVER...

NOW, I'M ABOUT TO KILL EVERY HUMAN HERE...

THEY'VE CAUSED ME TOO MUCH TROUBLE.

SO WHAT'S IT GONNA BE?

BUT THESE TWO DIE, OF COURSE.

...I'M WILLING TO SPARE THE PEOPLE OF COCO VILLAGE.

WHAK!

UNH...

...YOU CAN SEE WHAT A TRAGIC MISTAKE THAT WOULD BE!!

GULP....!!

OR STICK WITH THESE WEAKLINGS AND TRY TO FIGHT ME TOGETHER!!

BUT IF YOU LOOK AT THE SHAPE THESE TWO ARE IN...

COME BACK TO ME NOW AND SAVE YOUR BELOVED VILLAGERS...

ARE YOU MY SHIP-MATE...

WELL, NAMI!!?

...OR THEIRS?

BUT IF I SAY I'M ARLONG'S, ALL OF THE VILLAGERS WILL BE SPARED!! IS IT UP TO ME TO DECIDE WHO LIVES AND WHO DIES!!?

IF I SAY I'M LUFFY AND ZOLO'S SHIPMATE, EVERYONE MAY GET KILLED.

I HAVE TO BELIEVE IN THEM!!!

THAT'S DIRTY!! HE'S GONNA KEEP NAMI NO MATTER WHAT SHE DECIDES!!

...!!

BUT...I...

OKAY!!!!

...WITH ME!!!

FIGHT AND DIE...

I'M SORRY, EVERYONE!!!

DO OM!!

FWUP!

ZOLO...

THAT'S PLENTY!!

SPLASH!!

THIRTY SECONDS!! I WON'T LAST MORE THAN THAT.

CHOMP

COULD IT BE THAT RUBBER BRAT!!?

ARLONG PARK HAS NO FOUNTAINS!

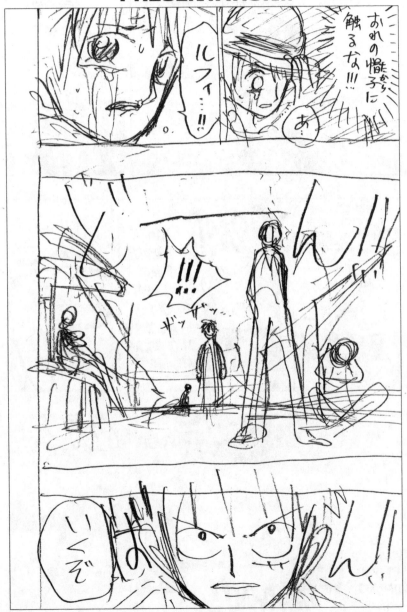

Chapter 89:
TRADE-OFF

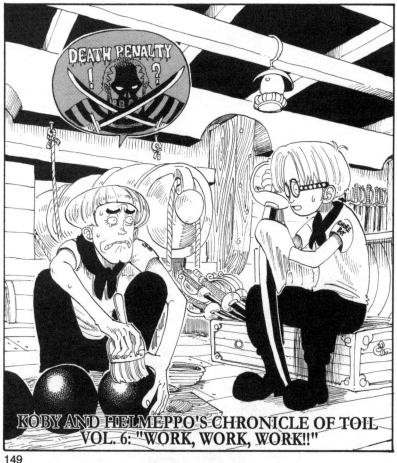

KOBY AND HELMEPPO'S CHRONICLE OF TOIL
VOL. 6: "WORK, WORK, WORK!!"

IF I CAN JUST KICK THE ROCK AROUND LUFFY'S LEGS TO PIECES, HE CAN SWING INTO ACTION !!!

HE'S THE ONLY ONE LEFT WITH ANY HOPE OF BEATING ARLONG !!!

GLUB GLUB GLUB

IT'S BROTHER COOK!!! I DON'T KNOW WHAT HE'S DOING DOWN THERE, BUT WE'RE ALL COUNTING ON HIM NOW!!!

BROTHER ZOLO!! HOLD FAST!!

SO IF THAT BRAT IS STILL ALIVE, THEN SOMEONE...

...BUT THE OCEAN ALSO TAKES AWAY THEIR WILL TO LIVE.

NOT ONLY DO PEOPLE WITH DEVIL-FRUIT POWERS LOSE THEM UNDER-WATER...

...MUST BE HELPING HIM!!!

HUH!!?

shake

shake...

WHOA!! THE OCTOPUS GUY IS GETTING UP!!

LOOK OVER THERE!!

BLINK!!

...!!

WHAT'S HE GONNA DO?

WHAT!!?

THWUMP!!

WHAAAT!!?

DARN!! I THOUGHT A RUBBER BAND WAS COMING AT ME!!!

DOOM!!!

ba-bump ba-bun

OCTOPUS...

wheeze wheeze

YOU AIMED AT ARLONG.

HA HA HA HA HA

SEE!? I SCARED HIM!!!

LEAVE THE REST TO ME!!!

GLUB

GLUB

!

FWUP

GET BACK!!! I CAN SHATTER THAT ROCK.

GLUB

A FISH-MAN!

!!

JUST ONE GOOD KICK !!!

WHOOM!!!

DIE!! DIE!!!

HEH
HEH...

WHEEZE

EH?

RRM **MMBB** I'D
BETTER
...

...FINISH HIM
OFF RIGHT
NOW!!!

...WOULD'VE
KEPT SOME
OF THE
WOUNDS
FROM
OPENING
UP!!!

.....

LYING
STILL
...

HUFF HUFF

!

I MEANT
OCTOPUS
BOY.

I
WASN'T
TALKING
ABOUT
ME!!

IS THAT
YOUR
IDEA
OF A
JOKE
?

YOU'RE
PROB-
ABLY
RIGHT.

HUH!!!?

I TOLD YOU. THIS IS OUR GAME... AND WE'RE WINNING.

WHAT!?

PLOO

!!!?

GRAAAAR!!!!

THAT WAS CLOSE!!!

KA-BAM!!!

WHOA.

...!!

blup blup...

IT'S THE RUBBER BOY!!!

FWWP?

PHEW...

......!!!

LUFFY!!

BROTHER LUFFY!!!

IDIOT!!!

IT'S ABOUT TIME...

THE RUBBER BOY.

·····

UH-UNH...

GASP

IT DIDN'T WORK!!!

NOOOOU

KLAK KLAK KLAK...

SHIVER-

!!!?

DID YOU... DO SOMETHING?

RRMMMMBB..

I'M GONNA... KILL HIM!!

WUMP

JUST WARMING UP.

KRAK KRAK

YEP.

Q: After reading your manga, Sensei, I'm inspired to follow my dream. My dream is to build a big bridge in America.

A: That's nice. A young man with dreams. I like that. All right then, do it. And if anyone gets in your way I'll go and--wearing hard leather boots--stomp on the pinky toe of his foot, so don't worry. Go for it.

Q: Knock, knock, Oda Sensei. Oda-body home!!?

A: Give me a break.

Q: When Patty the Cook says "I'm turniply saucy," what does it mean?

A: "I'm terribly sorry." He tends to make things sound like food. For example, he might say: "He's quite a man. He did lettuce of ham-glazing a-cheese-mints. Peas apple-aud him." But if *you* say things like that, people will probably look at you funny.

Q: A question for you. Is there a bone in Usopp's nose? I've seen it bend so many times. Like *squish*.

A: I've never seen that. Bend...like *squish*? How absurd...

Whoa!! It does bend!!!
Here ends SBS!!

Chapter 90:
WHAT CAN YOU DO?

KOBY AND HELMEPPO'S CHRONICLE OF TOIL
VOL. 7: "CHORES, CHO--!!?"

BUT YOU'D HAVE BEEN BETTER OFF DYING PEACEFULLY AT THE BOTTOM OF THE OCEAN.

HA HA HA HA HA... HOW TENACIOUSLY YOU SCUM HOLD ON BY YOUR STUBBY LITTLE TEETH.

UNH!!

UNH!!

WOING WOING

CAN'T YOU UNDER-STAND WHY I'M UPSET?

I'M GLAD THEY RESCUED ME.

UNH!!

I'LL SOON MAKE YOU WISH FOR A QUIET DEATH.

I'VE WATCHED MY BELOVED COMRADES BE DEFEATED BY WORMS!!!

HEY, WHERE DID BROTHER ZOLO FLY OFF TO!?

ALL OF HIS FEROCIOUS ATTACKS DIDN'T EVEN SEEM TO FAZE ARLONG!!

IS BROTHER LUFFY ALL RIGHT?

.....

EWIK
EWIK
EWIK

BIG DEAL.

THWUMP!

GO, LUFFY!! I'VE GOT YOUR BACK!!

KROOSH
SPLASH

YOU'RE RIGHT.

THAT WOULD BE THE END OF THE EAST BLUE.

IF LUFFY LOSES, WE'RE ALL DEAD.

WHUP

WEBBED TOES !!?

I... I THINK HE'S SERIOUS.

IS BROTHER LUFFY JOKING !?

HUP.

NO-- SPECIES !!!!

CHONK!! CHONK!! CHONK!! CHONK!!

OOF! UNH! OH! WAH!

GRAAR!!

KRAS...!!

WAAAAAAH!!! HE CHEWED UP THAT STONE PILLAR!!!

THOOM!!

WOW!! SCARY!

HE'LL BE EATEN UP, BONES AND ALL!!

AAAAAAH

IF THOSE JAWS CLAMP ONTO LUFFY, THEY WON'T JUST LEAVE MARKS.

...!?

FROM THE MOMENT OF BIRTH, AN UNBRIDGEABLE GULF SEPARATES OUR SPECIES !!!

SUPER-HUMAN STRENGTH IS THE BIRTHRIGHT OF ALL FISH-MEN.

YOU'RE INHERENTLY INFERIOR!!!

THE HEAVENS DIDN'T SMILE ON YOUR PUNY KIND IN THAT REGARD.

...

!? **KRAK!!**

THAT'S NOTHING.

SO WHAT !!?

HE'S RIGHT! AND NO HUMAN CAN SPAN THAT GULF NO MATTER HOW HARD HE TRAINS!

...TO CRUSH STONE.

DO—OM!!

YOU DON'T HAVE TO HAVE BIG TEETH...

TWITCH!! IT'S POINTLESS TO ARGUE.

THOON!! THAT'S RIGHT!! YOU SHOWED HIM!!

HA HA!! GOOD ONE, BROTHER !!!

YOU SINK LIKE ROCKS IN THE OCEAN!!! WHAT CAN YOU DO !!?

HUMANS ARE A STUPID, WEAK, FOOLISH SPECIES !!!

...BUT I HAVE FRIENDS WHO WILL RESCUE ME!!!

MAYBE I CAN'T DO ANY-THING...

KLINK

DOES HE EVEN KNOW HOW TO USE A SWORD?

SHOO!!

FWOOS

UNH
!!!

KLAK KLAK

KLAK...!!!

ENOUGH
FOOLISH-
NESS.

CLENCH
YOUR
TEETH
!!!

FWRRR...

WHOOSH

WHAT
!!?

DOOM!!

GWAAAAH!!!

HE SHATTERED ARLONG'S TEETH !!!!

HUH? WHAT'S HE ON ABOUT?

THOOM

SPLASH

I DON'T KNOW HOW TO USE A SWORD, SHARK FACE !!!

DOOM!

.....

I DON'T KNOW HOW TO NAVIGATE EITHER!!!

I KNOW I CAN'T LIVE WITHOUT HELP FROM A LOT OF PEOPLE!!!

HEY.

AND I CAN'T TELL LIES!!

FWUP

I CAN'T COOK!!

.....

WHAT A BURDEN IT MUST BE FOR YOUR CREW TO HAVE SUCH AN IDIOT FOR A CAPTAIN.

I DON'T KNOW WHY THEY FIGHT SO DESPERATELY TO SAVE YOU.

BWAH HA HA HA HA... WHAT A CLEVER BOY YOU ARE TO ADMIT YOUR OWN HELPLESS-NESS!!!

AN ENDLESS NUMBER OF TIMES!!!

KRA

AN ENDLESS NUMBER OF TIMES!!!

SHEENK

WOW.

THIS IS A SPECIAL POWER BESTOWED BY THE GODS.

.....

CHOMP!!!

...HOW SUPERIOR WE FISH-MEN ARE?

NOW DO YOU SEE...

BROTHER LUFFY-Y-Y!!!

L-LORD ARLONG! THAT HURTS!!!

WHAT?

COMRADE!!!

PHEW...

FWUMP!!

TWITCH

TWITCH

WHY YOU LITTLE GUM-GUM...

HEY! I JUST THOUGHT OF SOMETHING FUN!

TO BE CONTINUED IN *ONE PIECE*, VOL. 11!

Luffy's fun idea makes him more than an ideal match for the
toothsome Captain Arlong. During a brief lull in their pitched

IN A SAVAGE WORLD RULED BY THE PURSUIT OF THE MOST DELICIOUS FOODS, IT'S EITHER EAT OR BE EATEN!

"The most bizarrely entertaining manga out there on comic shelves. *Toriko* is a great series. If you're looking for a weirdly fun book or a fighting manga with a bizarre take, this is the story for you to read."
—*ComicAttack.com*

TORIKO

Story and Art by *Mitsutoshi Shimabukuro*

In an era where the world's gone crazy for increasingly bizarre gourmet foods, only Gourmet Hunter Toriko can hunt down the ferocious ingredients that supply the world's best restaurants. Join Toriko as he tracks and defeats the tastiest and most dangerous animals with his bare hands.

You're Reading in the Wrong Direction!!

Whoops! Guess what? You're starting at the wrong end of the comic!

...It's true! In keeping with the original Japanese format, **One Piece** is meant to be read from right to left, starting in the upper-right corner.

Unlike English, which is read from left to right, Japanese is read from right to left, meaning that action, sound effects and word-balloon order are completely reversed... something which can make readers unfamiliar with Japanese feel pretty backwards themselves. For this reason, manga or Japanese comics published in the U.S. in English have sometimes been published "flopped"– that is, printed in exact reverse order, as though seen from the other side of a mirror.

By flopping pages, U.S. publishers can avoid confusing readers, but the compromise is not without its downside. For one thing, a character in a flopped manga series who once wore in the original Japanese version a T-shirt emblazoned with "M A Y" (as in "the merry month of") now wears one which reads "Y A M"! Additionally, many manga creators in Japan are themselves unhappy with the process, as some feel the mirror imaging of their art skews their original intentions.

We are proud to bring you Eiichiro Oda's **One Piece** in the original unflopped format. For now, though, turn to the other side of the book and let the journey begin...!

–Editor